'N SYNC BACKSTAGE PASS

Your Kickin' Keepsake Scrapbook!

by Michael-Anne Johns

SCHOLASTIC INC.

New York   Toronto   London   Auckland   Sydney   Mexico City   New Delhi   Hong Kong

Photography credits:
Front cover: Anthony Cutajar; Back cover: Anthony Cutajar/London Features; 1: Anthony Cutajar ; 3: C. Stiefler/Famous; 4: Nick Tangley/Retna; 6: Eddie Malluk; 7: Bernhard Kuhmstedt/Retna; 8: Anthony Cutajar; 9: Bernhard Kuhmstedt/Retna; 10, both: C. Stiefler/Famous; 11, top: Jon Super/Retna; 11, bottom: Anthony Cutajar; 12–14, all: Bernhard Kuhmstedt/Retna; 15: Anthony Cutajar; 16, top: C. Stiefler/Famous; 16, bottom: Bernhard Kuhmstedt/Retna; 17, left: Bernhard Kuhmstedt/Retna; 17, right: Pierre ZonZon/South Beach Photo Agency; 18, left: Anthony Cutajar; 18, right: Arjan Kleton/Famous; 19: Bernhard Kuhmstedt/Retna; 20: Bernhard Kuhmstedt/Retna; 21: Anthony Cutajar; 22, left: Bernhard Kuhmstedt/Retna; 22, right: Pierre ZonZon/South Beach Photo Agency; 23, left: Anthony Cutajar; 23, right: Bernhard Kuhmstedt/Retna; 24, top: Bernhard Kuhmstedt/Retna; 24, bottom: Nick Tangley/Retna; 25, both: Bernhard Kuhmstedt/Retna; 26: Eddie Malluk; 27, top: Nick Tangley/Retna; 27, middle: Janet Macoska/Retna; 27, bottom: Nick Tangley/Retna; 28, top: Bernhard Kuhmstedt/Retna; 28, bottom: Pierre ZonZon/South Beach Photo Agency; 29, top: Anthony Cutajar; 29, bottom: Larry Busacca/Retna; 30: Nick Tangley/Retna; 31: Anthony Cutajar; 32, top: Bernhard Kuhmstedt/Retna; 32, bottom: Larry Busacca/Retna; 33, both: Bernhard Kuhmstedt/Retna; 34, top: Rudi Trueck/Famous; 34, bottom: Bernhard Kuhmstedt/Retna; 35, left: Larry Busacca/Retna; 35, right: Bernhard Kuhmstedt/Retna; 36: C. Stiefler/Famous; 37: Anthony Cutajar; 38, both: Bernhard Kuhmstedt/Retna; 39, left: C. Stiefler/Famous; 39, right: Eddie Malluk; 40, both: Bernhard Kuhmstedt/Retna; 41: Anthony Cutajar; 42, left: Pierre ZonZon/South Beach Photo Agency; 42, right: Fred Duval/Famous; 43: Anthony Cutajar; 45: Anthony Cutajar; 46: C. Stiefler/Famous; 48, bottom: Anthony Cutajar/London Features.

ISBN 0-439-07224-7

Cover design by Madalina Stefan
Interior design by Keirsten Geise

12 11 10 9 8 7 6 5 4 3 2 1   9/9 0 1 2 3 4/0
Printed in the U.S.A.
First Scholastic printing, February 1999

1

'N SYNC

'N THE BEGINNING

Justin Timberlake, **Chris Kirkpatrick, Joey Fatone, Jr., Lance Bass**, and **JC Chasez**: Five young guys who *aren't* related, *didn't* grow up together, and *weren't* recruited by a music manager, meet by chance in Orlando, Florida. They're all talented, all busy paying their showbiz dues, all ambitious. Bonus: they've become friends.

In 1995, they decide to form a band.

By 1998, they are 'N Sync, a worldwide, platinum-selling mega-group. Sound simple? Reality check: not.

'N COMING: get 'n step and 'n tune with 'N Sync's startling story of success. It doesn't get any sweeter than this.

FLASHBACK, 1991: *The New Mickey Mouse Club*

Back when cable's The Disney Channel hit the airwaves, one of its first variety shows was *The New Mickey Mouse Club*, a remake of a successful 1950's children's TV show. The '90s version, quickly dubbed *MMC*, was a combination of music, dance, comedy skits, and short films. It featured a dozen 'tween and teen "Mouseketeers," who were excellent dancers, singers, actors, *and* comics.

So what's that got to do with 'N Sync? Three words: JC, Justin, and Joey!

JC Chasez, all of 15 years old and an aspiring entertainer, traveled from his family's home in Maryland to try out for *MMC*. Good move: he was cast on the spot, and quickly became a fan favorite. Aside from singing and dancing, JC acted the part of Clarence "Wipeout" Adams on the show's weekly drama, *Emerald Cove*.

Justin Timberlake, then only 12 years old, joined the show in 1993. A native of Memphis, Tennessee, Justin was already an accomplished dancer and singer who'd won a local "Dance Like the New Kids on the Block" contest. The youngest member of *MMC*, he, too, became an instant fan-magnet — and, more important, a friend of JC's.

Joey Fatone, Jr. wasn't an *MMC* cast member — exactly. The Brooklyn, New York, born babe began his showbiz career when he was 13, and his family moved to Orlando. He not only snagged small roles in movies and the TV show *seaQuest*, he also performed regularly in Universal Studio's *Beetlejuice Graveyard Revue*. Joey had one other, *smaller* gig: he was an extra who danced during the closing song on *MMC*. That's how he hooked up with Justin and JC.

Chris Kirkpatrick was a kid from Pittsburgh

> **POINT OF VIEW!**
> "We're like brothers — definitely.
> We grew up together."

GETTING 'N SYNC!

WHEN 'N SYNC FIRST GOT TOGETHER, THEIR ONSTAGE TRAINING INCLUDED DANCING FOUR TO FIVE HOURS IN A HOT WAREHOUSE, SO THEY COULD BUILD UP THEIR STAMINA.

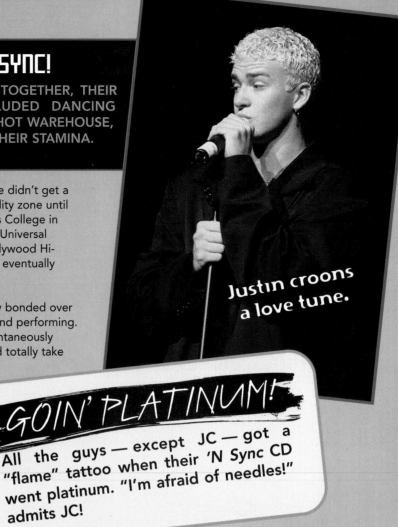

Justin croons a love tune.

who always wanted to be a singer. He didn't get a chance to kick his dream into the reality zone until after high school: he attended Rollins College in Orlando. There, he got a job — with Universal Studios' music and dance group, Hollywood Hi-Tones. At that gig, he met Joey, who eventually introduced him to Justin and JC.

So, at first, there were four. They bonded over everything, including music, dance, and performing. When they'd go to clubs, they'd spontaneously erupt in mad-crazy dance moves, and totally take over the dance floor. Soon, regular patrons were asking, "Who's the group with the mad moves?"

THE NAME GAME

It was Chris's idea to pick up on what people were already assuming, and form an actual group. Their strength would be singing, which they already did on *MMC* and at Universal Studios — and naturally, dancing.

The others agreed to give it a shot. They also agreed on a need: one more member to help handle harmonies. Justin had been working with a vocal coach for several years, and that's who suggested **Lance Bass**, a former client, who once toured with a Mississippi singing group called Attache.

And so the early wheels for 'N Sync were 'n motion: not that they had a name just yet.

It was Justin's mom who thought it up. "We thought it was a good name to represent us," Justin revealed to *Teen Beat* magazine, "because it described our personalities, our singing, and our dancing all in one. Shortly after we copyrighted it, we recognized that the last letters of our names [including Lance's nickname, Lansten] spelled 'N Sync."

GOIN' PLATINUM!

All the guys — except JC — got a "flame" tattoo when their 'N Sync CD went platinum. "I'm afraid of needles!" admits JC!

WORKIN' IT

Okay, so they're a group, with a name. That and an E-ticket would get them on all the rides at Disney World — but not much more. To be a successful group means to make albums, and to tour. And to do that, as any wanna-be rock star knows, means signing up with a record company. To make *that* happen, it helps much to have a professional manager. 'N Sync's quest was clear.

So they worked it: Instead of clubbing after punching out of their day jobs, they'd rehearse, going to midnight, or later. "Plus, during any break we got, we'd be doing just vocal rehearsals," JC described. "We didn't take it lightly. We knew what we wanted to do and we concentrated on it."

Next step was paying for time in a recording studio and making a "demo" — short for demonstration tape, to send out to potential managers. Because 'N Sync has to be seen to be appreciated, the boys took it to another level. JC continues the saga: "We performed at Disney World's Pleasure Island, and videotaped the whole thing. That's the package we sent — our demo tape and our videotape — to different managers and record companies."

THE BACKSTREET CONNECTION

Though lots of pros were interested in 'N Sync, it was the mastermind team behind another Orlando pop group, Backstreet Boys, who picked up on the band. The plan was to use the same strategy that had worked for BSB: break 'N Sync overseas first — in the *more* dance-pop-friendly climes of Europe, Asia, Australia, and Canada — *then* bring 'em back to the USA as certified hitmakers.

On the real, it worked. A German record deal was secured first, and "I Want You Back" proceeded to tear up the charts all over Europe, followed quickly by "Tearin' Up My Heart." Two versions of their self-titled CD came out — one for Europe; the other for Canada.

SMOOTH MOVES

By the end of 1996 'N Sync was ready to take on their home shores. They signed with RCA Records for an American multi-CD deal, and dropped their good-luck first single "I Want You Back" on February 13, 1998. Their American *'N Sync* CD followed on March 24, 1998. It debuted on *Billboard*'s Top 200 chart at no. 44 and climbed up into the Top 5. By the summer of 1998, *'N Sync* was multi-platinum, which means it sold millions!

As their singles and videos got constant radio and MTV airplay, 'N Sync made plans to take America by

Hunks in trunks! Joey, Lance, Justin, Chris, and JC cool off!

New Year's Eve 1998. It seemed as if 'N Sync was every-where, on the road, on the radio, on MTV! They appeared in other TV specials such as the annual Macy's Thanksgiving Day parade, and the December airings of the *Disney Channel Christmas Special*, *ABC Walt Disney*

'N SYNC CONFESSION-SESSION!

Joey: "My bad habit is that I talk too much."

JC: "*I talk too much on the phone.*"

Chris: "Sometimes I ignore somebody during a talk. It's bad, I know, but when I'm not interested, I'm just not listening."

Lance: "Bad habits? . . . I don't remember. It seems that I have a bad memory."

storm. The band made TV appearances — from an 'N Sync concert on the Disney Channel to the Ricki Lake chat show. They took their moves on the road and opened for Janet Jackson's "Velvet Rope" tour during the last two weeks of October 1998. Right before Thanksgiving 1998, they began their own headlining tour, which lasted until

World Christmas Special and *A Kathie Lee Christmas*, plus hosted ABC-TV's live TGIF party when the new season began.

In early 1999 'N Sync returned to Europe and Asia for a major world tour — and they released their second European CD. And the beat goes on. . . .

Turn the page for the personal and up close peep at 'N Sync.

2

JUSTIN RANDALL TIMBERLAKE

"JUSTIN"

He may be the baby of the band, but Justin Timberlake is an experienced pro. Born on January 31, 1981, in Memphis, Tennessee, Justin was seven years old when he and his mom, Lynn, moved to Orlando, Florida. Justin's parents were in the middle of a divorce, and his dad stayed back in Memphis. At first it was hard on the little boy — he missed his dad — but his mom worked hard to make the change as easy as possible.

Justin had always loved performing, and soon after the move he began entering contests. He was in a "Dance Like the New Kids on the Block" competition — and he won. A few years later, Justin signed up for piano and guitar lessons, and began to study with a vocal coach. He was always in some school play or local talent show. When he was 12 years old, Justin was cast as a member of TV's The New Mickey Mouse Club. "It was a great opportunity," he says. But perhaps the best thing that happened because of MMC was that Justin hooked up with his 'N Sync pals. Today, Justin admits, "My life is like a fairy tale. Every day I receive about five hundred fan letters. It feels great to be liked."

JUST JUSTIN

Full Name: Justin Randall Timberlake
Group Nicknames: Justin, Curly, The Baby, Mr. Smooth, Bounce
Birthdate: January 31, 1981
Zodiac Sign: Aquarius
Birthplace: Memphis, Tennessee
Childhood Hometown: Memphis, Tennessee
Current Residence: Orlando, Florida
Hair: Blond
Eyes: Blue
Height: 5'11"
Parents: Lynn and Randall
Siblings: Half brothers, Jonathan and new baby Steven, courtesy of his dad and stepmom
Pets: A dog named Ozzie; a cat named Alley

Musical Influences: Boyz II Men, Babyface, Blackstreet, Jimi Hendrix
Group Role: The reliable one
Collections: Sneakers; University of North Carolina basketball gear
Fantasy Career Goal: "To be a basketball player like Michael Jordan."
First Date: "I took a girl to the movies."
First Kiss: "It was when I was ten with my girlfriend. I was in the sixth grade and she was in the eighth grade — I've always been into older women! [But] I was thirteen when I had my first *real* kiss. Mindy was a girl who also worked at the Disney Studios.

It was at a friend's birthday party. It was like there was nothing else in the universe but us."
Ideal Girl: "Pretty is cool, but it's not really about looks for me. It's more about personality. I like a girl with a good sense of humor, who's humble, and sensitive."
Hobbies: Singing, dancing
Sports to play: Basketball
Worst Habits: Burping and constantly clearing his throat
Boxers or Briefs: Calvin Klein briefs
Innie or Outtie: Innie

Justin and his mom, Lynn. "She's the strongest person I know," he says.

TOTAL HIGH!

"I love the feeling when you're up there onstage singing and the crowd is getting into what you are doing. I love to see smiles on their faces and know that I had something to do with that."

Justin shows off h broken thumb— casualty of an onstage mishap.

He's number ONE!
He's number ONE!

Justin was named the 'N Sync fave-rave in a German teen magazine.

FAVES

Fun Time: Shopping

TV Show: *Friends* — "But I don't get to watch it too much, because we've been on the road so much."

Movies: *The Usual Suspects, Scream, Ferris Bueller's Day Off*

Actors: Brad Pitt, Tommy Lee Jones, Jim Carrey

Actresses: Sandra Bullock, Meg Ryan

Model: Tyra Banks

Dream Girl: Jennifer Aniston

Singers: Notorious B.I.G., Stevie Wonder

Spice Girls: Mel B and Emma Bunton

Author: John Grisham

Singers/Groups: Brian McNight, Take 6

Music: R&B, hip-hop

Car: Red Mercedes-Benz

Foods: Healthy foods, and cereal — especially Apple Jacks and Cap'n Crunch; pasta

Snack: Chocolate chip and Daiquiri Ice ice cream

Colors: Baby blue, hunter green, royal blue

Holiday: Christmas

Sport: Basketball

Sports Team: University of North Carolina's basketball team, the Tarheels; Chicago Bulls; Orlando Magic

Sports Superstar: Michael Jordan

Word: Crunk (it means crazy or cool)

Animal: Dog

Vacation Spot: Hawaii

DISLIKES

* People who have mad mood swings and are phony.
* The fact that he's impatient and procrastinates.
* Snakes!
* His curly hair.
* Smoking of *any* kind.
* Getting up in the morning — he won't say a word until he eats his cereal!

WISH UPON A STAR!

"If I could have a super power, it would be to fly."

EXTRA TIDBITS
* Justin was totally red-faced when he broke his thumb while he was performing onstage. It hurt, too.
* Though he's the baby of the band, Justin's fellow 'N Syncers named him the Most Mature and Most Reliable in the group.
* Justin can't pass a mirror without checking himself out. "Yes, I will confess to that," he told a reporter, but it's not conceit. It's because, for years, he had trouble controlling his curly hair!

JOSHUA SCOTT CHASEZ

"JC"

His name is Joshua, but for as long as he can remember, he's been JC. He was born in Washington, DC, on August 8, 1976. His parents, Roy and Karen, soon moved the family, which included younger sibs, Heather and Tyler, to Bowie, Maryland. Growing up, JC played sports, especially football and basketball, and he loved to sing and dance. He wasn't really thinking of a career in showbiz, but when a friend suggested he go to an open audition for the Disney Channel's *The New Mickey Mouse Club*, JC checked it out. Before he could sing, "M * I * C * K * E * Y M * O * U * S * E," he won a spot in the cast.

Of his time with *MMC*, JC says, "It was really great. It helped to prepare me for what I'm doing now. We filmed several shows every week, so I'm used to a heavy work schedule. Also, we produced an album and toured quite a bit, so I already knew what life on the road was all about. The other really cool thing is that I met Joey and Justin through *MMC*, so I guess you could say that *MMC* is responsible for 'N Sync getting together. It just seems like fate that we all came together like we did. You never know where your friendships might lead you."

THE JUICE ON JC

Full Name: Joshua Scott Chasez

Group Nicknames: "JC," Mr. Casual, Big Daddy

Birthdate: August 8, 1976

Zodiac Sign: Leo

Birthplace: Washington, DC

Childhood Hometown: Bowie, Maryland

Current Residence: Orlando, Florida

Hair: Brown

Eyes: Blue-hazel

Height: 6'1"

Parents: Karen and Roy

Siblings: Brother, Tyler (T.J.); sister, Heather

15

Wonder what lucky fan got JC's stuffed Dalmation?

Ethnic Origins: English and French
Musical Influences: Sting, Seal, Stevie Wonder
Group Role: JC is considered the "Daddy" because he looks out for the other guys — makes sure they eat enough and get rest.
Collection: Hard Rock Cafe menus
What He Sleeps In: Calvin Klein pajamas
Briefs or Boxers: Tommy Hilfiger boxers
Shoe Size: 11
First Job: A Mouseketeer on *The New Mickey Mouse Club*
First Kiss: "It was in the first grade, but I want to keep her name private 'cause later, I went out with her for three years."
First Date: "It was at a party. I met one girl and we danced together. I didn't leave her all night long."
Ideal Girl: "She has to be sincere."
Hobbies: Singing, dancing, writing music
Sports to play: Football, in-line skating, swimming
Worst Habit: JC sleeps every chance he gets!
Innie or Outtie: Innie

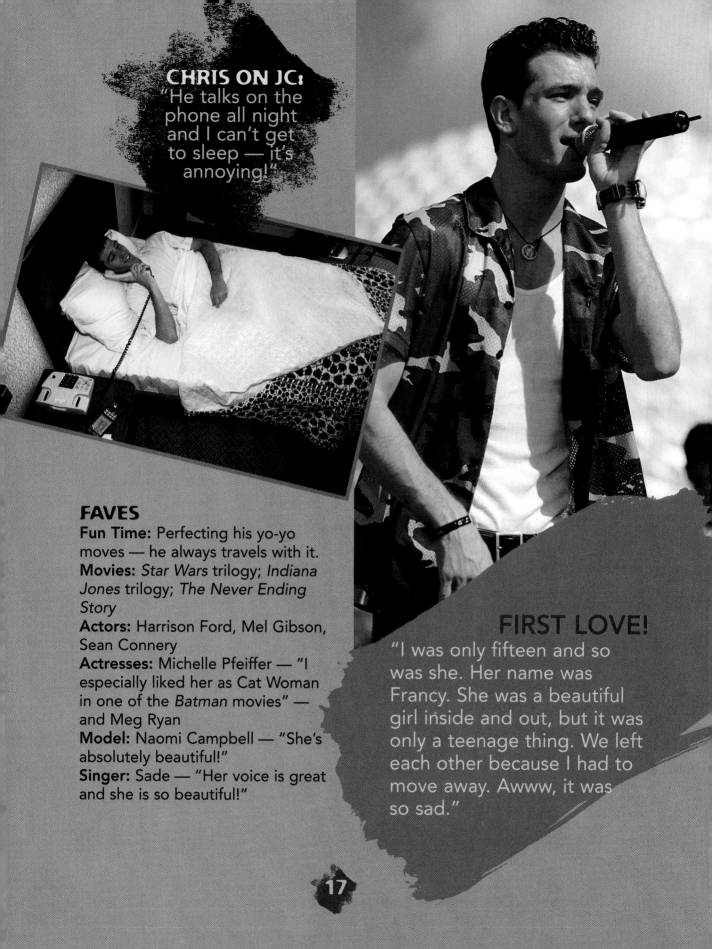

CHRIS ON JC:
"He talks on the phone all night and I can't get to sleep — it's annoying!"

FAVES
Fun Time: Perfecting his yo-yo moves — he always travels with it.
Movies: *Star Wars* trilogy; *Indiana Jones* trilogy; *The Never Ending Story*
Actors: Harrison Ford, Mel Gibson, Sean Connery
Actresses: Michelle Pfeiffer — "I especially liked her as Cat Woman in one of the *Batman* movies" — and Meg Ryan
Model: Naomi Campbell — "She's absolutely beautiful!"
Singer: Sade — "Her voice is great and she is so beautiful!"

FIRST LOVE!
"I was only fifteen and so was she. Her name was Francy. She was a beautiful girl inside and out, but it was only a teenage thing. We left each other because I had to move away. Awww, it was so sad."

Singing Group: Boyz II Men
Car: Jeep
Food: Chinese
Snack: Ice cream — mint chocolate chip or chocolate chip cookie dough
Drink: Water

CHILDHOOD MEMORY

"When I used to play hide-and-go-seek in the laundry pile and I would feel so safe because I could smell my parents. It sounds funny, but I used to sit in there, and you do, you just feel so comfortable because you feel close to your mom and dad."

Spice Girl: Scary Spice — "She's one cool chick! I met her a while ago in Germany, and she liked our new single 'Tearin' Up My Heart' — she loved it!"
Friends **Star:** "Courteney Cox — she's the one for me! I got into her first when she was in *Ace Ventura*."
Classic Literature Author: William Shakespeare

Color: Black
Holiday: Christmas
Clothes: "My leather jacket"
Personal Possession: Walkman
Sport: football
Sports Team: Washington Redskins

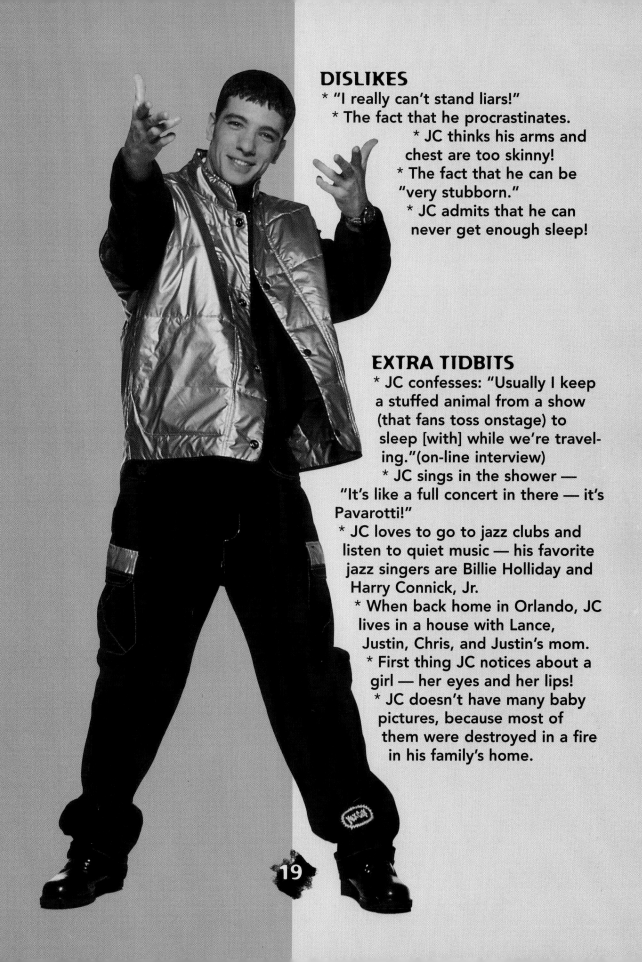

DISLIKES

* "I really can't stand liars!"
* The fact that he procrastinates.
* JC thinks his arms and chest are too skinny!
* The fact that he can be "very stubborn."
* JC admits that he can never get enough sleep!

EXTRA TIDBITS

* JC confesses: "Usually I keep a stuffed animal from a show (that fans toss onstage) to sleep [with] while we're traveling."(on-line interview)
* JC sings in the shower — "It's like a full concert in there — it's Pavarotti!"
* JC loves to go to jazz clubs and listen to quiet music — his favorite jazz singers are Billie Holliday and Harry Connick, Jr.
* When back home in Orlando, JC lives in a house with Lance, Justin, Chris, and Justin's mom.
* First thing JC notices about a girl — her eyes and her lips!
* JC doesn't have many baby pictures, because most of them were destroyed in a fire in his family's home.

19

4

JOSEPH ANTHONY FATONE, JR.

"JOEY"

Joey Fatone, Jr. was born in Brooklyn, New York, on January 28, 1977. Joey is proud of his Italian heritage. And like many talented sons of Italy before him (Frank Sinatra, John Travolta, and Joey's musician father, Joe Fatone, Sr.) Joey loved to perform for an audience. At the age of 3 Joey was already putting on shows for his family and friends, and he had the lead role in his kindergarten production of *Pinocchio.*

When Joey was 13, his parents, Joe Sr. and Phyllis, moved the family to Orlando, Florida. It was a major break for the teen-aged up-and-coming entertainer. Almost immediately, Joey landed TV commercials, guest spots on TV series like *seaQuest,* and even a role in *Once Upon a Time in America* with his idol Robert De Niro. After Joey graduated from

Dr. Phillips High School in Orlando, he landed a job at the Universal Studios theme park. He played Dracula and the Wolfman in the *Beetlejuice Graveyard Revue*. Meanwhile, over at the rival theme park, Disney World, JC and Justin were getting their "mouse ears." When the guys eventually met, a lifetime friendship was born.

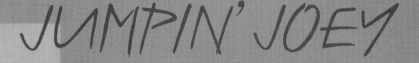

JUMPIN' JOEY

Full Name: Joseph Anthony Fatone, Jr.
Group Nicknames: Joey, Phat-One, Mr. Flirt
Birthdate: January 28, 1977
Zodiac Sign: Aquarius
Birthplace: Brooklyn, New York
Childhood Hometown: Brooklyn until he was 13, then Orlando, Florida
Current Residence: Orlando, Florida
Hair: Brown
Eyes: Hazel
Height: 6' 1"
Parents: Phyllis and Joe
Siblings: Sister, Janine; brother, Steven

High School: Dr. Phillips High School in Orlando
Ethnic Origins: Italian

Ideal Girl: "A fun girl with a great personality who enjoys company, is honest, and can take a joke. She should like going to the movies. I like people who aren't afraid to speak their mind"
Most Romantic Place: "Lake Eola in Florida— they have swans and these boats you can pedal and go out on the lake."
Hobbies: Going to the movies, video games, Jet Skiing
Sports to play: In-line skating (but he doesn't like sports very much)
Worst Habit: Burping in public — he admits it!
Wildest Fantasy: "I don't know! I guess just a big pool of Jell-O — that's all I'm gonna say!"
Innie or Outtie: Innie

Musical Influences: His dad, Joe Sr. — "he used to sing in a group called the Orions. They weren't famous, but they were great." Also Frankie Lymon and the Teenagers, and Boyz II Men.
Group Role: Cheerleader — he keeps the guys' spirits up.
Collection: Superman memorabilia — T-shirts, jewelry, anything and everything
Briefs or Boxers: Briefs — Fruit of the Loom
First Date: "I don't remember. I think it was in New York and we went to the movies."

Joey and his proud parents, Phyllis and Joe.

DISLIKES
* Phonies
* His own feet. "They are too big! I step on people's feet everywhere I go!"
* Joey hates being kidded about his snoring!

FAVES
Fun Time: Playing video games, going to parties and clubs — and dancing!
Cartoon Character: Superman
Movies: *Billy Madison*, *My Life*
Actor: Robert De Niro
Actress: Jodie Foster
Dream Girl: Demi Moore
Song: Boyz II Men's "Water Runs Dry"
Spice Girl: Well, ex-Spice Girl — Geri "Ginger" Halliwell
Classic Literature Author: William Shakespeare
Foods: Italian — especially his mom's lasagna
Drink: Pepsi
Color: Purple
Holiday: Christmas
Clothes: "My Superman hockey jersey."
Word: Bur-r-r-r-t (said loudly and unexpectedly!)
Animal: Black panther
City: London — "There's a real buzz about the city."

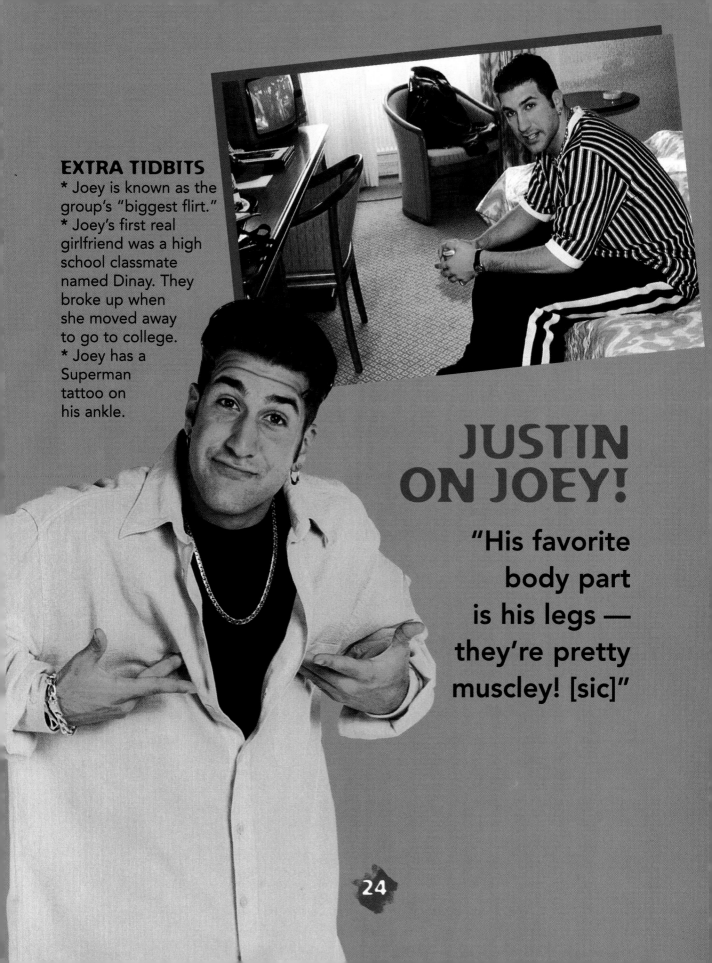

EXTRA TIDBITS
* Joey is known as the group's "biggest flirt."
* Joey's first real girlfriend was a high school classmate named Dinay. They broke up when she moved away to go to college.
* Joey has a Superman tattoo on his ankle.

JUSTIN ON JOEY!

"His favorite body part is his legs — they're pretty muscley! [sic]"

"No matter what I do,
I go at it full tilt
and can't be stopped."

MR. SUNSHINE!

"I'm always happy. I'm the flirtatious, happy-go-lucky one of the band. If someone's down, I try to get him or her in a good mood — that's my charm! I have to look on the bright side of everything."

5

'N SYNC

FACT OR FICTION?

Test Your 'N Sync 'N Stinct. Check Out These Tabloid Tidbits and See If You Know the Difference Between Rumor and Real!

1. JC isn't concerned about other people's problems. He just wants to succeed himself.

Fiction! As a matter of fact, JC is very concerned about the living conditions of others and feels as a celebrity he should give back to others who aren't as lucky as he is. "There are too many people who have been born into bad situations," JC mentioned in a magazine interview. "They need a chance to get out."

2. Chris is having emotional problems — there are even stories going around he's seeing a psychologist.

Fiction! Maybe this rumor started because he majored in psychology in college. Duh!

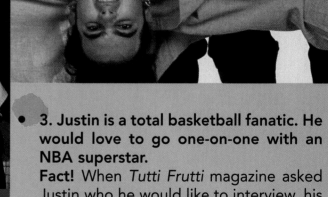

3. Justin is a total basketball fanatic. He would love to go one-on-one with an NBA superstar.

Fact! When *Tutti Frutti* magazine asked Justin who he would like to interview, his hoop dreams were revealed when he answered: "Probably Anfernee [Penny] Hardaway because that's my boy — he's from Memphis! I'd ask him what he plans to do with his basketball career in the future."

27

4. Fame has gone to Joey's head, and he's only in 'N Sync for the money.

Fiction! Conceited? The guy who thinks his feet are too big? Hardly! Down-to-earth Joey loves performing for people, and if he can succeed in a career as an entertainer, cool! His goals are pretty simple. "In ten years I see myself having a nice home," he told *Teen Party* magazine. "I would love to have my own house. And I really want to see a 'Joey' 'N Sync doll. I want to be able to see myself and say, 'Hey, that's *me* as a doll!' "

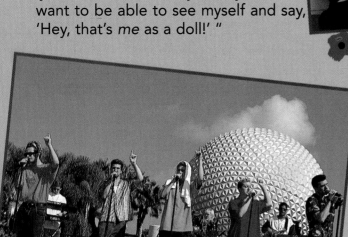

5. Justin is the fans' favorite member of 'N Sync, and that makes Lance, Joey, JC, and Chris very jealous. It's so bad they could break up any day now.

Fiction! Each member has a huge contingent of fans, so there is no competition between them. When this rumor was brought up during an April 1998 AOL online chat, they all laughed and JC commented, "It's all good." Joker Chris added, "Justin's *our* favorite too!"

6. 'N Sync is very conscious not to use swear words — on or off stage.

Fact! Joey explained to a fan during a Canadian Much Music radio interview: "We really don't [cuss]. But, there's a game that we play if we accidentally do. Um, it's pretty funny. It's like, if you happen to curse, you have to say 'noogie' and if you don't say 'noogie,' everybody gets to punch you until you say it! It keeps us in line, you know, tryin' not to swear!"

7. The guys in 'N Sync are real animal lovers. They even brought a dog on the road during their spring 1998 German concert dates.

Fact! "We're adopting a dog over in Germany and at the end of the tour we're giving it away to a fan," Lance told *Teen Beat* before they left for Europe. "We want to go to a shelter where they keep pets . . ." Justin started to explain until Lance cut in with: "I was watching *Lifestyles of the Rich and Famous*, and I saw this girl who started an adopt-a-pet organization in America. A lot of celebrities who love pets get the dogs and cats that are about to be put to sleep and give them to people. So we want to do that in Germany. I want exotic animals too — maybe a ferret." Justin had a thought about that — "No reptiles whatsoever! I will not ride the tour bus if there are reptiles!"

8. Chris almost had to leave 'N Sync when he got braces.

Fiction! But he *was* worried about it. Chris told a dj from Canada's Much Music, "When I first had them put on, the group was together for a little over a year. I was afraid because they were cumbersome and I thought when we were in the studio, you could hear a change in my 'S's' or something like that. But it was only when I wore the retainer — like to sleep at night — that you could hear my 'eshes shtart to shound like thish!' "

9. Lance's parents didn't mind him leaving high school to join 'N Sync.

Fact! But *with* a condition! "They were all for it," he told *Teen Beat*. "Once they saw it was really happening, they knew they weren't going to stop me." That did not mean Lance could just forget about his diploma, though. "So I finished school through independent study through the University of Nebraska."

10. Justin is always late and he's constantly holding up the other guys when they are on tour.

Fiction! Except it *used* to be true. Justin admitted to *BOP* magazine that he *used* to be the major hold up because of his curly hair. "I tried to brush my hair, but that doesn't work on my curls. Now I just throw some gel in it, slick it back, and then just kind of mess it up real quick. Ever since I started being able to work with my hair, well, that's when I started getting ready faster." He also confessed that he learned to shorten his shower time, and now he can be up and out the door in fifteen minutes!

6

CHRIS ALAN KIRKPATRICK

"CHRIS"

The oldest member of 'N Sync, Chris Kirkpatrick was born October 17, 1971, in Clarion, Pennsylvania. Chris' dad died when he was still in grade school. Understandably, that was the worst day of Chris' life. His mom, Beverly, was a single parent until she remarried. Now Chris is a big brother to four half sisters, Molly, Kate, Emily, and Taylor.

As a child, Chris loved to make people laugh, but it wasn't until he was in high school that he realized he wanted to be a performer. His drama teacher cast Chris as the lead in a school production of the musical *Oliver!* and all at once the teenager knew what he wanted to do for the rest of his life.

Throughout high school, Chris performed in plays and musicals. However, when he enrolled in Rollins College in Orlando, Florida, he decided to major in psychology, another huge interest. But he didn't give up his dream of being a singer. When he was 21, he won a role with Universal Studios' music and dance group, Hollywood Hi-Tones.

Though Orlando is visited by millions of tourists, for the locals it is something of a small town. Everyone seems to know everyone else, so it wasn't so surprising that Chris would eventually meet up with JC, Joey, and Justin and come together to form 'N Sync.

DAREDEVIL!

Do not try this! Chris admits that he once really took his life in his hands when he "surfed in a hurricane."

CHRIS' COMPUTER PRINTOUT

Full Name: Christopher Alan Kirkpatrick
Group Nicknames: Chris, Lucky, Crazy
Birthdate: October 17, 1971
Zodiac Sign: Libra
Birthplace: Clarion, Pennsylvania
Childhood Hometown: Pittsburgh, Pennsylvania
Current Residence: Orlando, Florida
Hair: Brown
Eyes: Brown
Height: 5'8"
Parents: Mother, Beverly
Siblings: Half sisters Molly, Kate, Emily, and Taylor

Worst Habits: Bites his fingernails and always forgets stuff in his hotel rooms

Most Embarrassing Onstage Moment: "When I only got halfway over in a flip we do, and I landed on my face!"

Innie or Outtie: Innie

FAVES

Fun Time: Dancing at clubs — especially to techno music!

Movie: *Mad Max*

Actor: Mel Gibson

Actress: Audrey Hepburn

Best Friend Outside of 'N Sync: "His name is Angelo, and he lives in L.A."

School Status: Graduated from Rollins College as a psychology major

Ethnic Origins: Scottish, Spanish, Irish, and Native American

Musical Influence: The Beatles

'N Sync Musical Role: Sings the falsetto (high) parts

Collection: Records

Briefs or Boxers: Calvin Klein or Tommy Hilfiger briefs

First Date: "My first date was with my baby-sitter. She was seventeen and I was a baby. Joke! But seriously, I had my first date when I was a kid. Her name was Kelly. We danced at a party."

Ideal Girl: "Has to have a great sense of humor and be very outgoing."

Hobbies: Writing songs on his laptop computer

Sports to play: Surfing, in-line skating, basketball, football, roller hockey

Most Valuable Possessions: Rollerblades and surfboard

Dream Girl: Gwen Stefani of No Doubt

Singers: Michael Jackson, Brian McKnight

Spice Girl: Victoria "Posh Spice" Adams

Singing Groups: Green Day, No Doubt

Foods: Mexican, especially tacos, and pizza

Snack: Chocolate ice cream

Drink: Orange juice

Colors: Black and silver
Holiday: Halloween
Clothes/Accessory: Jerseys and bandannas
Sport: Football
Word: Dude
Animal: Tiger
Childhood Memory: "Going to my grandma's house."
Vacation Spot: Cancún, Mexico

DISLIKES
* Looking at his fingernails when he's bitten them all the way down.
* "I have a really short attention span, so things tend to bore me easily, which I hate."
* His feet — Chris thinks they are too small.
* Broccoli

A SUIT-'N'-TIE KINDA GUY ... NOT!

"I'm definitely a jeans and T-shirt type of guy. A couple of years ago, we had a picture of us in these different-colored suits, and everyone looked great — except me!"

EXTRA TIDBITS

* Chris wears very little jewelry — just silver earrings (two holes in each ear) and a silver chain.
* Chris would love to meet . . . "Mozart. He was a genius. I'd like to know how he thought and where he drew his inspiration from."
* If Chris is ever missing in action, you can usually find him at the beach, his favorite place on earth.
* Chris has two lucky numbers — 7 and 17.
* Chris wears glasses sometimes.
* Chris performed in the Hollywood Hi-Tones show at Universal Studios in Orlando.
* Chris got his braces off in 1998 — "I smile all the time now!"

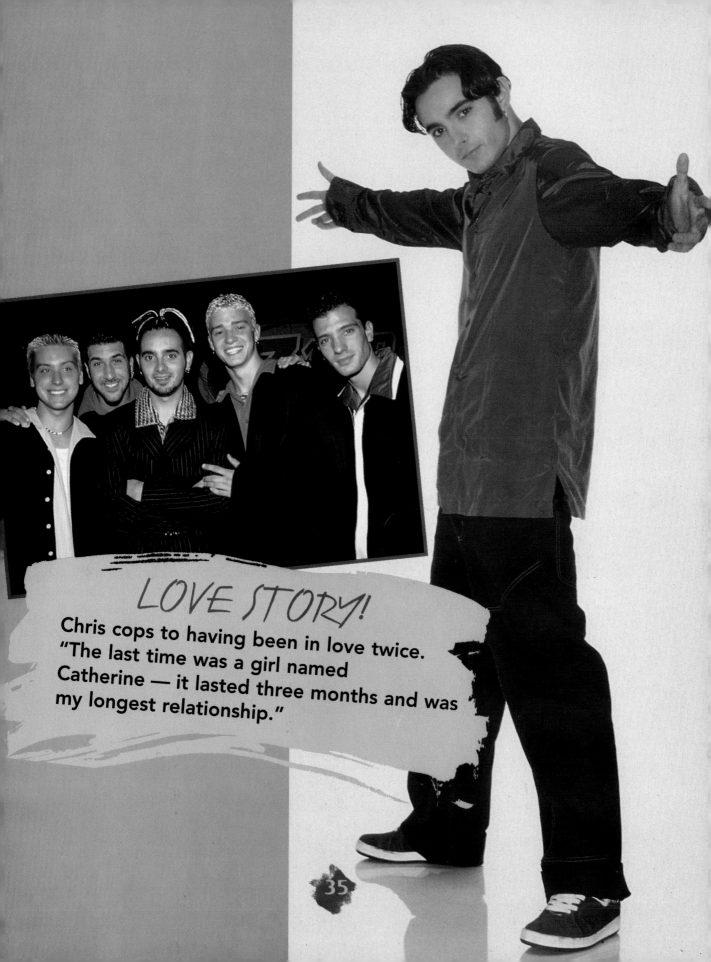

LOVE STORY!

Chris cops to having been in love twice. "The last time was a girl named Catherine — it lasted three months and was my longest relationship."

7

LANCE BASS
"LANSTEN"

When James Lance Bass was born on May 4, 1979, his older sister, Stacy, declared he was a little doll. She had no idea that 20 years later, half of the world's female population would agree with her!

When Lance was 11 years old, his family moved from their hometown of Laurel, Mississippi, to the nearby town of Clinton. In the seventh grade, Lance joined his school's chorus, and a year later he auditioned for, and won, a spot in the statewide chorus, Mississippi Show Stoppers. Lance also joined a competition choir called Attache, which toured all over Mississippi.

Music was always Lance's first love, but for a time, he considered pursuing a career working with the astronauts at NASA. He even passed the NASA entrance exam. But, in 1995, Lance jettisoned all thoughts of outer space. That's when he got a phone call from a former voice coach. The teacher wanted to introduce the young singer to four Floridians who were putting a group together. Lance flew to Orlando, met Justin Timberlake, Chris Kirkpatrick, JC Chasez, and Joey Fatone, Jr., and, as they say, the rest is history!

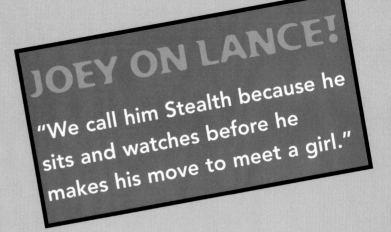

JOEY ON LANCE!

"We call him Stealth because he sits and watches before he makes his move to meet a girl."

THE LOWDOWN ON LANCE

Full Name: James Lance Bass
Group Nicknames: Lansten, Mr. Cool, Scoop — "Because I always know what's going on!"
Birthdate: May 4, 1979
Zodiac Sign: Taurus
Birthplace: Laurel, Mississippi
Childhood Hometown: Clinton, Mississippi
Current Residence: Orlando, Florida
Hair: Blond
Eyes: Blue (but sometimes look hazel)
Height: 5'10"
Parents: Jim and Diane
Siblings: Sister, Stacy

School Status: Sophomore in college, and plans on majoring in business management

Ethnic Origins: Native American, English

Musical Influences: Garth Brooks, Boyz II Men

'N Sync Musical Role: Bass singer

Collection: Tazmanian Devil merchandise, old comic books, stamps

Briefs or Boxers: Boxers

First Job: "I dressed up like a big dog named 'Poofoo.'" In that guise, he worked for a company that made personalized books by computer. It was Lance's job to go around and take pictures with the kids.

First Career Goal: To work with NASA

Best Birthday: When the group was in Africa

First Kiss: Bethany Dukes, when he was in kindergarten

First Date: "I went dancing with friends and met a girl there. It was cool."

Ideal Girl: Adventurous, fun-loving, affectionate, cute

Hobbies: Playing video games, weight training

Sports: Karate, horseback riding

Car: Dodge Stealth

Dream Tour Partner: Mariah Carey or Paula Abdul

Dream Duet Partner: LeAnn Rimes, Madonna, Janet Jackson

Dream House: Horse ranch

Innie or Outtie: Innie

FAVES

Fun Time: Going to the beach, rock climbing, skydiving
Cartoon Character: Tazmanian Devil
TV Shows: *Friends, Mad About You*
Movie: *Mortal Kombat Annihilation*
Actor: Tom Hanks
Actresses: Jennifer Aniston, Lucille Ball
Spice Girl: Mel C
Modern Author: Elie Wiesel
Classic Literature Author: William Shakespeare
Singing Groups: Boyz II Men, Offspring
Singer: Garth Brooks — "I love his song 'The Dance.' I like him so much because of the way he performs, and the show he puts on. We'd like to remake 'The Dance' someday."

Car He Dreams of Owning: Toyota 4-Runner
Foods: French toast, pizza
Drink: Dr Pepper
Color: Candy apple red
Holiday: Christmas
Jewelry: "I wear the watch and the necklace from our manager. We all have them and are proud of them because he gave them to us for our first gold record. The ring on my left hand, I got from a girl. My name is engraved in it. Every time I wear it, I remember my home."
Clothes: Old army suspenders and sweater
Ideal Girl: "I like wholesome type girls — Miss Teen USA type girls!" (By the way, Lance was at the Miss Teen USA Pageant at the time he said this. He also confessed, "I fell in love fifty-one times today!")
Getaway Place: Beach

Lance and his mom, Diane.

DISLIKES
* His hair because, "It's too thick!"
* "People who prejudge us."
* His habit of biting his nails.
* The fact that he's messy and never cleans his room.
* When he talks and no one listens!
* Mushrooms

MOMMY DEAREST!

On Mother's Day 1998, Lance's mom, Diane Bass, was interviewed on a radio show and gave up the 411 on her son. "Actually, Lance is a good kid — he's never done a lot of crazy things, but about two weeks ago, he did something really crazy. He was in Cancún, and went to a bullfight and they asked for volunteers from the audience. He raised his hand and volunteered. And he actually got out there! I think that after it was all over with, he realized that might have not been a real good idea, but he wasn't thinking at the time. But he survived it — thank goodness."

EXTRA TIDBITS
* Compliments make Lance blush.
* Lance's earliest memory is his uncle's wedding.
* Lance once worked as a vocal coach.
* Lance's most embarrassing moment was when he did an impression of a squirrel eating a nut at a party.
* If Lance could change one thing about himself, he says, "I would want to be taller."

8

'N SYNC FAQS*

* Frequently Asked Questions

Q: Have any of the 'N Sync guys had his heart broken?
A: Justin, for one, remembers: "The producers of the *Mickey Mouse Club* gave a huge party, and I met a viewer who had won an invitation. We got on right from the start. I was head over heels in love. She was my first [big] love. We dated for nine months. But at the end of 1995 it was over. I had made a terrible discovery. She cheated on me with someone else. That's when my world ended. You cannot imagine how hurt and disillusioned I felt. I never want to be humiliated like that again . . . I tried to forgive her. But she didn't want me anymore and she broke up with me. It took me six months to get over it." (European magazine *Joepie*)

'N Sync goof on their manager, Johnny Wright.

Q: Do Justin, JC, Joey, Chris, and Lance ever argue?
A: Occasionally. Says Justin, "Sometimes we get on each other's nerves. We argue about hairstyles, clothing, who gets to talk to a girl first — Joey always wins that one. He's definitely the flirt of the band."

Q: How would Lance describe himself?
A: "I try to keep a good attitude about everything," he told *Teen Party* magazine. "I mean, I hardly ever get mad about anything. I just try to stay friendly."

Q: If Joey could relive any moment in his life, what would it be?
A: "My senior year in high school," he confessed to *Teen Party* magazine. "I had the most fun and everybody, the whole senior class, were all together and tight. It was just the best experience I had. Seeing everyone when they were freshmen and thinking back on all the things you did. When you go to that final day at graduation, it's just the biggest sigh of relief."

Q: What was the funniest or most embarrassing thing that happened to 'N Sync onstage?
A: "I broke my thumb onstage once," Justin revealed during an AOL on-line chat. "We were doing an outdoor show, and the set was wet. We do this dance move where we slide across the stage. I just slid a little too far, my hand hit the stage, and my hand buckled. And I still finished the song!"

Q: How do the guys envision themselves when they are older?
A: The guys all had answers to this question when they were interviewed at the BRAVO radio station birthday party in Poland. (They didn't know they had so many fans in Poland until this trip!)
Chris: "But I'm already older . . ."
Lance: "I'll be a grandpa. I hope I'll have a wife, children, and then grandchildren. I'd love to have a lot of free time. I hope I'll visit many countries."
Joey: "I hope that I'll have a wife, a couple of kids, and a house someday. I'd like to have fun and travel a lot with my wife and kids."
Justin: "I'll never grow old — I'm just joking! It's hard to say. When I'm older, I want to be able to look over my shoulder and say with pride that I've done many things in my life. Of course, I wanna have a wife and children, too."

Chris [again]: "I'll not get married probably, 'cause there isn't any girl who will take me!"

Q: How does 'N Sync stay grounded?
A: "We have each other to keep in check," Chris noted in an August 1998 AOL chat. "If someone gets out of focus a bit, there's always the other guys to bring you back."

Q: Would any of the guys in 'N Sync ever date a fan?
A: "That's hard to say," Chris told a fan during their August AOL chat. "If given the opportunity, I don't know why not."

Q: Will fame change the 'N Sync guys?
A: Justin took that query on a Canadian Much Music radio interview. "No. We started as 'N Sync, and we'll always be 'N Sync. I don't think our personalities will change. We always try, in every way we can, to stay as close to our fans as possible. But sometimes our schedule gets really busy. I'll give you a 'for instance.' We'll be at an autograph signing and, you know, we stayed an hour late, and we missed our sound check. But we have to leave and make it to the venue for the show. That disappoints us sometimes. But our fans are here for us and we appreciate them. That's why we do this."

9

BATTLE OF THE BOY BANDS!

'N SYNC vs BACKSTREET BOYS

"Okay, so are you the *new* Backstreet Boys?"

Justin, Lance, JC, Joey, and Chris have heard this question about a gazillion times. It is a reasonable query since 'N Sync and the BSB seem similar in many ways. Both feature five furiously talented fellas. Both call Orlando, Florida, home; both shared the same management team, *and* both have followed a similar strategy for success — breaking out in Europe *first*, then coming home to conquer this country. As a matter of fact, there have been reports that BSB's Nick, A.J., Brian, Howie, and Kevin were a little miffed when manager Johnny Wright seemed to be trying to clone them with N' Sync. In the very beginning, some critics were calling 'N Sync "Backstreet Boys lite."

Now both have topped the popularity polls, but that hasn't quieted some of the talk. Some say this success has one megagroup *pitted* against the other. BSB loyalists feel that 'N Sync's out to usurp BSB. 'N Sync fans claim BSB are out to squash 'N Sync. Is there enough room on the charts, and in fans' hearts, for both bands? Or is there a real Battle of the Bands brewing? You make the call — with a little help from 'N Sync themselves.

The real:
Yo! 'N Sync and BSB are friends! Got it?!!

Is 'N Sync trying to be just like Backstreet Boys and trying to beat them on the charts?

Chris: "No. We're just 'N Sync. We can both be [out] there. Both groups are doing great now. But we are smart enough to stay realistic and we don't expect that after the success of 'I Want You Back' it will be like this forever. It can all be over soon." (*Break Out* magazine)

What makes you different from Backstreet Boys?

Chris: "I like Busta Rhymes!"
Lance: "Our personalities and our live show. . . . I think we're just five totally different guys."
Chris: "We're more R&B."

A lot of people mix the two groups up — after all, you do look a lot like BSB. . . .

Lance: "Okay, we are five guys, too. We are also from Orlando. We [had] the same manager and we make music. But that's where the resemblance ends. . . . We are five *friends* who got into this business. We did it ourselves."
   (*Break Out* magazine)

Don't fans come up and say, "I like 'N Sync better than Backstreet Boys," or the reverse?

Lance: "That's like a total European thing. America is totally different because you can like both."

Justin: "This is our message to the whole 'N Sync/BSB debate. You can like both and it's okay."

(KIIS-FM radio, Los Angeles, CA)

How can you be friends with BSB and still compete with them?

Joey: "You probably won't believe it, but we don't see Howie, Brian, A.J., Kevin, and Nick as our competition. We are really good friends now. We run into each other a lot. Sometimes we see them in Orlando. . . during TV shows, in hotels, or in airplanes. We always have lots of fun."

Justin: "We used to [go out together], but now all ten of us are very busy and we're always on the road. So we don't really get the chance to go out [much]. But if we are in Orlando, we meet and go dancing in a club or something."

(*Break Out* magazine)

What makes 'N Sync different from all *other* boy groups?

JC: "I think it's just because we're ourselves and people can appreciate the fact that we're ourselves. We like to have a good time and everybody wants to have a good time with us."

Joey: "It's making music as well. I mean, it's the love for music, the love of performing out there in front of all the fans and everything. Having a good time!"

Chris: "I think the choreography is really key. When you see our show, you'll see that we dance with every song — except for one *a cappella* song. When we sing, we like to dance, we like to move around and we show that onstage. There's even a dance break where all we do is dance. It's a lot of fun."

(Much Music Radio, Canada)

Is it true that 'N Sync and BSB are going to work on a CD together?

Maybe. 'N Sync opened for a few of the U.S. dates of Backstreet Boys' 1998 summer tour. At a recent charity basketball game, they were purposely teamed on the same side. As for working together on a project, however, that's looking less likely since Backstreet Boys are no longer with the same management as 'N Sync.

'N SYNC DISCOGRAPHY

'N SYNC

European Debut CD
1. "Tearin' Up My Heart"/ 2. "You Got It"/ 3. "Sailing"/ 4. "Crazy for You"/ 5. "Riddle"/ 6. "For the Girl Who Has Everything"/ 7. "I Need Love"/ 8. "Giddy Up"/ 9. "Here We Go"/ 10. "Best of My Life"/ 11. "More Than a Feeling"/ 12. "I Want You Back"/13. "Together Again"/ 14. "Forever Young"

'N SYNC

Canadian Debut CD
1. "Tearin' Up My Heart"/ 2. "I Just Wanna Be With You"/ 3. "Here We Go"/ 4. "For the Girl Who Has Everything"/ 5. "God Must Have Spent a Little More Time on You"/ 6. "You Got It"/ 7. "I Need Love"/ 8. "I Want You Back"/ 9. "Everything I Own"/ 10. "I Drive Myself Crazy"/ 11. "Crazy for You"/ 12. "Sailing"/ 13. "Giddy Up"

'N SYNC

US version of the debut CD was released in March 1998
1. "Tearin' Up My Heart"/ 2. "I Just Wanna Be With You"/ 3. "Here We Go"/ 4. "For the Girl Who Has Everything"/ 5. "God Must Have Spent a Little More Time on You"/ 6. "You Got It"/ 7. "I Need Love"/ 8. "I Want You Back"/ 9. "Everything I Own"/ 10. "I Drive Myself Crazy"/ 11. "Crazy for You"/ 12. "Sailing"/ 13. "Giddy Up"

HOME FOR CHRISTMAS

Released in the US on November 10, 1998
1. "The First Noel"/ 2. "The Christmas Song"/ 3. "This Christmas/ 4. "Holy Night"/ 5. "I Never Knew the Meaning of Christmas"/ 6. "Love's in Our Hearts on Christmas Day"/ 7. "Under My Tree"/ 8. "I Hear Angels"/ 9. "Will You Be Mine This Christmas"/ 10. "It's Christmas"/ 11. "In Love on Christmas"/ 12. "Home for Christmas"

US SINGLES/VIDEOS
"I Want You Back"/ "Tearin' Up My Heart" (released only for radio airplay)/ "God Must Have Spent a Little More Time on You"

"I Want You Back"

JC recalls the first time they heard this song, which would eventually be the first single they released. "It was August 1996, and we had just signed our record contract a week earlier. All of a sudden we were in Sweden meeting with three really famous songwriters — Denniz Pop, Max Martin, and Kristian Lundin — who write for a lot of other pop artists like Ace of Base and Robyn.

"The song is about suddenly finding yourself separated from the person you feel so deeply about because you've done something stupid to screw it up. I think it hits [people] because they can relate to it like a love song, but it's powerful and up tempo enough to kick them too."
(Teen People)

QUICK CUTS

* The US 'N Sync CD went platinum in August '98; the European and Canadian versions went *double* platinum!
* "I Want You Back" went gold in all markets!
* "I Want You Back" debuted on the *Billboard* pop chart at no. 25!
* American videos "Tearin' Up My Heart" and "I Want You Back" became heavy hits on MTV!
* 'N Sync's "Giddy Up" is included on the Geffen Records release of the CD *Music From Sabrina the Teenage Witch*. Also on the soundtrack is the Spice Girls' "Walk of Life," Robyn's "Show Me Love," and cuts from Backstreet Boys, Chumbawamba, and even the TV show's star, Melissa Joan Hart!

A SAD FAREWELL

Denniz Pop, the Swedish producer who worked with 'N Sync on their first songs, passed away during the summer of 1998. It was a great loss to JC, Justin, Chris, Lance, and Joey, and to the world of music.

"My favorite 'N Sync song is 'God Must Have Spent a Little More Time on You.' "
— Justin in an AOL chat

GET CONNECTED!

HOW TO REACH OUT & TOUCH 'N SYNC

FAN MAIL ... EMAIL ... VOICE MAIL!

WHEW, there are certainly enough ways to get in touch with 'N Sync, and you'll find them all right here.

Official Fan Mail Address:
'N Sync
P.O. Box 692109
Orlando, FL 32869-2109

Record Label Address:
'N Sync
c/o The RCA Record Label
1540 Broadway, Times Square
New York, NY 10036

Official 'N Sync Web Site:
http://www.nsync.com

Official 'N Sync Fan Club Web Site:
http://www.nsync.com/fanclub/index.html

Some Crazy Cool Cyber Connections:
'N Sync's Fave Fashion Links
http://www.gap.com/
http://www.zoezone.com/

'N Sync's Fave Magazine Links
http://www.covergirl.com/
http://www.people.com

'N Sync's Fave Fun Links
http://www.thebox.com/
http://www.peeps.com/
http://www.disney.com/
http://www.mtv.com/

'N Sync Net-Surfing Links: Official Dutch 'N Sync Fan Club
http://www.geocities.com/SunsetStrip/
* lotsa info, pix, bios, interviews & articles (in English)

'N Sync Search Engine
http://jagnet.webjump.com/n-sync.html
* mega ways of getting in touch with 'N Sync fans and links

Ultimate Band List (UBL) http://ubl.com
* huge list of bands and musical artists

Send an Animated 'N Sync Message to Your Friends
http://www.nsync.com/index2.html
* Share a little 'N Sync today!

HUNT & PECK JOEY!
"I'm a horrible typist. I just like, plink, plink, plink, and before I know it, four hours are gone already."

JC CYBER CHAT!
"[When] I write back [on the Internet], all of a sudden I'll get like a billion hits the next day because I actually replied. I think it's brilliant. . .it's the bomb."

TRUE-BLUE JUSTIN!
"We love hearing from our fans. To know you've touched them enough that they listen to your songs so often that they know them by heart, that's special."

GET CHUMMY WITH CHRIS!
"I read all the email and I try to write back to as many as possible."

LINK UP WITH LANCE!
"I absolutely love talking to everybody. If I go on-line, like six hours pass, but you don't even know how long you've been on it."

Okay, Now You've Got the Connections. Send 'N Sync Your Personal Message and Let Them Know . . .

"YOU'VE GOT MAIL!"

12
WASSUP NEXT FOR

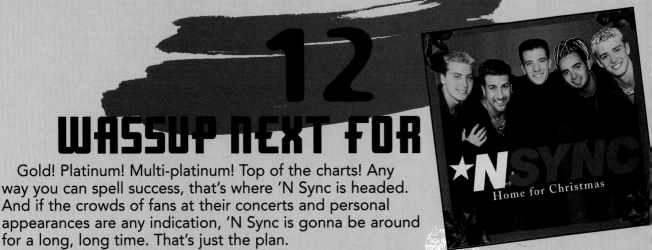

Home for Christmas

Gold! Platinum! Multi-platinum! Top of the charts! Any way you can spell success, that's where 'N Sync is headed. And if the crowds of fans at their concerts and personal appearances are any indication, 'N Sync is gonna be around for a long, long time. That's just the plan.

With their *Home for Christmas* CD hitting the stores for the 1998 holiday season, you might be surprised to know that 'N Sync already has a number of songs ready for their *next* European and American CDs. This time 'round, they are even more involved with their music than before. "We've kinda started writing songs," explains JC. "On our first album, we had only one original song. Hopefully, there'll be more of those on the next album."

But most of all, JC, Justin, Chris, Joey, and Lance want to continue doing what they've been doing all along — making music they love for the fans they love. "We want to be pioneers in the music industry," says Justin. "We want to make our own name. We have inspiration individually and as a group. We look up to groups like Boyz II Men, Take 6. . .but we just want to be 'N Sync."

MAJOR 1998 TV APPEARANCES

* *RuPaul* (VH1) — 6/6/98
* *'N Sync in Concert* (Disney Channel) — 7/18/98 (many repeats)
* *Late Night With David Letterman* (CBS) — 8/31/98
* *The Tonight Show Starring Jay Leno* (NBC) — 9/10/98
* 'N Sync was the "house band" for ABC's live TGIF party kicking off the 1998 fall TV season
* *Jenny Jones* (syndicated) — 9/28/98
* *Ricki Lake* (syndicated) — 10/23/98
* *Macy's Thanksgiving Day parade* — 11/26/98
* *Disney Channel Christmas Special* (with Shawn Colvin, Monica, and Usher) — 12/5/98
* *ABC Walt Disney World Christmas Special* — 12/25/98
* *A Kathie Lee Christmas* (CBS) — Christmas week 1998